LEILA SETH

WE, THE CHILDREN OF INDIA

THE PREAMBLE TO OUR CONSTITUTION

ILLUSTRATED BY

BINDIA THAPAR

PUFFIN BOOKS

An imprint of Penguin Random House

PUFFIN BOOKS

USA | Canada | UK | Ireland | Australia
New Zealand | India | South Africa | China

Puffin Books is part of the Penguin Random House group of companies
whose addresses can be found at global.penguinrandomhouse.com

Published by Penguin Random House India Pvt. Ltd
4th Floor, Capital Tower 1, MG Road,
Gurugram 122 002, Haryana, India

First published in Puffin Books by Penguin Random House India 2010

Text copyright © Leila Seth 2010
Illustrations copyright © Bindia Thapar 2010

Photographs on pages 6, 7, 13, 29, 30, 32, 33, 34-35 courtesy the Nehru Memorial Museum and Library, New Delhi.
Photographs on pages 9, 12 courtesy the India International Centre Library, New Delhi.

26

The views and opinions expressed in this book are the author's own
and the facts are as reported by him/her which have been verified to the extent possible,
and the publishers are not in any way liable for the same.

ISBN 9780143331513

Typeset in Perpetua by Abha Graphics
Printed at Aarvee Promotions, India

www.penguin.co.in

Leila Seth was the first woman judge of the Delhi High Court and the first women to be Chief Justice of a state in India. She retired as Chief Justice of Himachal Pradesh in 1992. She was a member of the 15th Law Commission of India and responsible for the report on Free and Compulsory Education of Children. She was involved in human rights activities and with a number of schools and colleges. She had a diploma in Montessori education. In 2003, her autobiography *On Balance* was published by Penguin to much critical acclaim. Leila Seth passed away in 2017 at the age of eighty-six.

Bindia Thapar was an architect by training and an illustrator by choice. She was best known for her wide variety of illustrations for children. Bindia Thapar passed away in 2014, after battling cancer.

Dear Children,

I have written this book about the Preamble to the Constitution of India for you. It has been written with the help of my grandchildren, Anamika, who is five years old, and Nandini, who is eight.

We believe that being a good citizen is very important. (A citizen is a person who belongs to a country.) This means following the goals of the Constitution. These goals are contained in the first long sentence, known as the Preamble. To be good citizens, we feel that we should understand the Preamble, so that its spirit becomes a part of us.

Republic Day 2010   LEILA SETH

The drawings in this book are dedicated to Smitu and are for Maow and Amit.

BINDIA THAPAR

Many years ago, perhaps even before your grandparents were born, India was a very different country to live in. The people of India could not always talk to whomever they wanted, or work wherever they wanted, or even decide what the rules to run the country should be.

All this was decided by the British, who had come from far away. They came as traders, but stayed on as rulers for about 200 years.

Many Indians were not happy about being forced by the British rulers to change their ways of thinking, studying and working. They were also unhappy that they were not allowed to do certain jobs or to go to certain places.

Some Indians got together and discussed how they could make the British leave. In the beginning they fought the British with guns and other weapons. Some people got hurt, some people died, but nothing much changed.

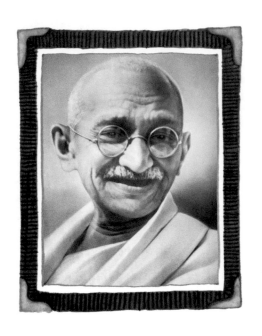

In the year 1869, Mohandas Karamchand Gandhi, whom we also know as Mahatma Gandhi or Bapu, was born in Gujarat. When he was in his twenties, he realized that being truthful and peaceful and brave were the best ways of bringing about change. He became the leader of the people who were trying to make India independent. He said that India could be freed not by fighting, but through Ahimsa, that is, by non-violent means. He suggested that we Indians should become self-reliant. We should think for ourselves and not follow orders from the British if we thought these orders were wrong.

Bapu walking on the beach in Bombay (Mumbai).

Jawaharlal Nehru speaking at midnight on 14 August 1947. In his speech he used the famous words 'a tryst with destiny', which means 'a meeting with fate'.

After many years of struggle, India became an independent country on 15 August 1947. From then onwards we have been a free country where we, the citizens (that is, the people who belong to the country), decide how the government is chosen and how it works—and how we can try to make our own and other people's lives better.

7

After we became independent, we decided to recognize certain things:

OUR NATIONAL ANTHEM, JANA GANA MANA

OUR FLAG, THE TRICOLOUR

OUR NATIONAL EMBLEM

OUR NATIONAL ANIMAL

OUR NATIONAL BIRD

OUR NATIONAL FLOWER

We also wrote a national book called the Constitution of India, which contains all the ideas and rules that keep our country working. This is the most important book in our country. It starts with the Preamble, which is the introduction. The Preamble is the soul of the Constitution. It sets out our national goals, such as justice and equality. (Justice means being just or fair.)

Let me now talk about what the Preamble says and what it means—and about how it came to be written and the people who wrote it.

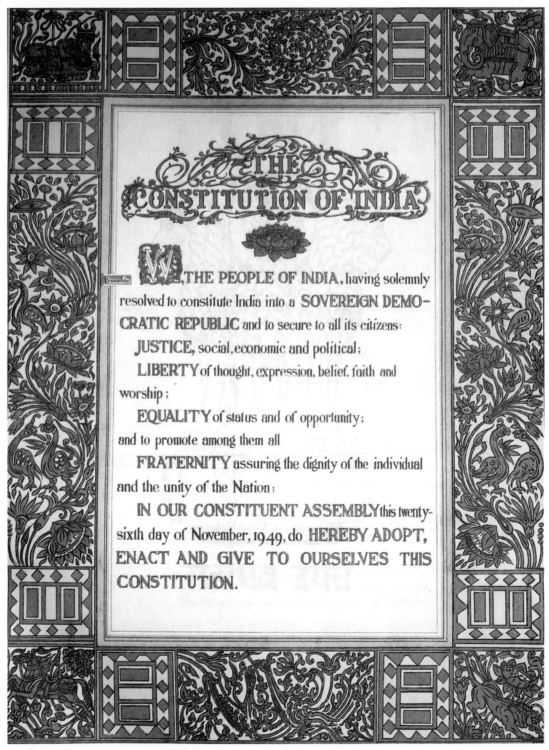

THE

CONSTITUTION OF INDIA

WE, THE PEOPLE OF INDIA, having solemnly resolved to constitute India into a SOVEREIGN DEMOCRATIC REPUBLIC and to secure to all its citizens:

JUSTICE, social, economic and political;

LIBERTY of thought, expression, belief, faith and worship;

EQUALITY of status and of opportunity; and to promote among them all

FRATERNITY assuring the dignity of the individual and the unity of the Nation;

IN OUR CONSTITUENT ASSEMBLY this twenty-sixth day of November, 1949, do HEREBY ADOPT, ENACT AND GIVE TO OURSELVES THIS CONSTITUTION.

The Preamble to the Constitution of India.

The Preamble was changed in early 1977 and the words SOCIALIST SECULAR were added, as well as the word INTEGRITY.

So the Preamble now reads—

The Fundamental Rights (or basic rights) of each citizen have always been a part of our Constitution, but the idea of Fundamental Duties was added in early 1977. These include defending our country, promoting brotherhood and sisterhood, taking care of forests, lakes, rivers and wildlife, and striving towards excellence.

WE, THE PEOPLE OF INDIA, having solemnly resolved to constitute India into a SOVEREIGN **SOCIALIST SECULAR** DEMOCRATIC REPUBLIC and to secure to all its citizens:

JUSTICE, social, economic and political;

LIBERTY of thought, expression, belief, faith and worship;

EQUALITY of status and of opportunity;

and to promote among them all

FRATERNITY assuring the dignity of the individual and the unity and **integrity** of the Nation;

IN OUR CONSTITUENT ASSEMBLY this twenty-sixth day of November, 1949, do HEREBY ADOPT, ENACT AND GIVE TO OURSELVES THIS CONSTITUTION.

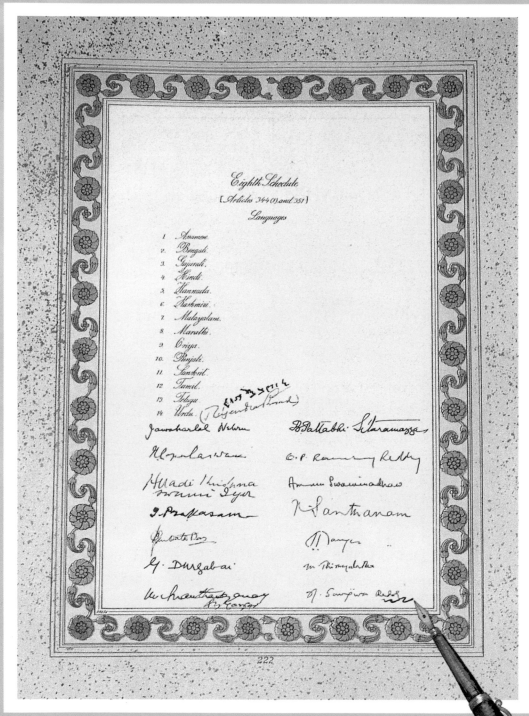

A page from the Constitution signed by Dr Rajendra Prasad, Jawaharlal Nehru and others.

In 1950, the Constitution was signed by our first President, Dr Rajendra Prasad, our first Prime Minister, Pandit Jawaharlal Nehru, and many others.

Jawaharlal Nehru was the first person to sign, and he was so excited that he did so without leaving any space for the President's signature! The President, however, managed to squeeze his signature above Pandit Nehru's.

Jawaharlal Nehru signing the Indian Constitution.

What, then, is a constitution?

It is a book that contains the ideas, rules, promises and duties agreed to by the people of a country. It can be changed from time to time if the citizens feel that it is necessary. But usually, because it is the most important law of a country, this cannot be done too easily.

India has a written constitution.

some countries (like Britain) don't have a written constitution.

In 1947, when India became independent of British rule, we decided what kind of life we wanted for ourselves as well as what rights and duties we should have. We also decided how we should be governed. We put our ideas together in the Constitution of India, which begins with the Preamble.

I am afraid the big words in the Preamble may look a bit unfamiliar at first. But it is well worth trying to understand them.

So now let us go over the Preamble. I will try to explain it in simpler words.

WE, THE PEOPLE OF INDIA: this includes all the people in our country, including children.

There are many languages in India that are only spoken, and don't have a written script.

India has about 1.3 billion people. We speak in many different languages, including twenty-two official ones.

There are about 400 million children below the age of fifteen in our country.

having solemnly resolved to constitute India into a:

having taken a firm decision to make India a:

SOVEREIGN: we, the citizens of the country, can alone decide what we want to do and no other country can tell us what to do.

Although no one can tell us what to do, we need to have agreements with other countries for trade, for keeping the peace, and to help solve certain problems such as climate change.

SOCIALIST: means that the people of a country should produce and share the country's wealth. Indira Gandhi, who was Prime Minister of India when this word was added to the Preamble, said that socialism meant 'bettering the life of the people of India'.

OM HINDUISM
JAINISM
CROSS CHRISTIANITY
ISLAM
JUDAISM
ZOROASTRIANISM
SIKHISM
BUDDHISM
BAHAI

SECULAR: in India we think of secular as meaning that the government should not prefer one religion to another. That is, all religions and beliefs should be respected equally and we should be free to practise the religion or belief of our choice. Religion should not be taught as a subject in government schools and there should be no government religion.

AGNOSTICISM ATHEISM RATIONALISM HUMANISM ANIMISM

Hinduism is the religion of
more than 80 per cent of Indians.

Christianity came to India
nearly 2000 years ago.

Islam is another religion that has been
followed in India for over 1000 years.

Some religions like Sikhism,
Buddhism and Jainism were
born in India. Buddhism spread
to many other countries
from India.

DEMOCRATIC REPUBLIC: means a government without a king or queen—which is run by people who are elected by the people for the good of the people.

Who makes our laws? Who runs our government?

Parliament is the name we give to the group of people whom we choose to make our laws. In India, Parliament consists of the Lok Sabha, the Rajya Sabha and the President. We elect 543 men and women to the Lok Sabha, and two are named without being elected. We elect 233 to the Rajya Sabha (but by a different method) and twelve are named without being elected. This makes a total of 790 Members of Parliament (MPs). The President is elected by quite a complicated method.

Every Indian who has reached eighteen years of age can
vote in an election to choose who should make our laws
and govern our country. It does not matter whether you are

a woman or a man,
or what your wealth,
education, caste or
religion is.

To vote is a way of
making your choice
for a person, thing
or idea. There can

be open voting or secret voting. When you choose the captain of your
team by the raising of hands, it is open voting. But when we choose
the people who make our laws, we have secret voting, so that we can
vote without any fear of upsetting anyone.

MPs discuss matters that affect the country and try and solve difficult
problems by creating new laws. After the Lok Sabha and Rajya Sabha have
each agreed to a suggested law, the final step is the President's signature.

The leader of the largest group of MPs in the Lok Sabha usually becomes
Prime Minister of India. The Prime Minister is the head of the government
of India and he or she chooses the ministers.

India is divided into states, such as Uttar Pradesh, Tamil Nadu and Gujarat.
In the states too, people are elected to make laws. The head of the
government of a state is called the Chief Minister, and she or he chooses
the ministers of that state.

The ministers run their governments with the help of people who are
known as civil servants. Some things are done by the Government of India,
some by the governments of the states, and some by both. The police help
to keep the peace inside the country, and the armed forces—that is, the
Army, Navy and Air Force—keep the peace outside.

and to secure to all its citizens: and to make sure that all its citizens get

JUSTICE, social, economic and political: means that people should be treated fairly and honestly in all matters. This includes (i) whether people around you behave well towards you, (ii) whether you are given an equal chance to earn your living and (iii) whether you can freely vote or be voted for.

safety

human rights

EQUAL OPPORTUNITY

dignity

LIBERTY of thought, expression, belief, faith and worship: means the freedom to do various things, including to speak and write openly about what one thinks; to live where one likes; to be free to choose one's friends; to choose and practise one's religion or belief; to travel; and to form groups—so long as one doesn't harm other people by doing so.

25

EQUALITY of status and opportunity: means that all citizens have to be treated in the same way no matter what their religion, place of birth, race or caste may be, or whether they are women or men, poor or rich. All of them must be given a chance to improve their lives.

and to promote among them all
FRATERNITY assuring the dignity of the individual and the unity and integrity of the Nation: means that all Indians should be encouraged to be like a family and take care of each other like brothers and sisters, despite their different languages, religions and cultures. This 'unity in diversity' is needed to make India strong.

IN OUR CONSTITUENT ASSEMBLY this twenty-sixth day of November, 1949, do HEREBY ADOPT, ENACT AND GIVE TO OURSELVES THIS CONSTITUTION: in our Constituent Assembly on 26 November 1949 accept and give to ourselves this Constitution.

Who helps to make sure that the government is run properly? The Courts, the Media, and all of us.

It is the work of the Supreme Court of India and the High Courts and lower courts of the various states to make sure that people get treated fairly and equally and that the laws are obeyed. The people who decide matters in the courts are judges, and it is their duty to be honest, fair and just.

The Media—which is what we call TV, radio, the Internet, newspapers and magazines—tell us what is going on in the country, what the government is doing, and sometimes how things can be improved.

And we ourselves, by reading, writing, discussing matters and speaking out, can form public opinion and bring pressure on the government to do what is right. Also, at the time of an election, if our MPs (or other people whom we have voted for) have not been honest or worked hard, we can vote for different ones.

NOW THAT WE HAVE TAKEN A RAMBLE THROUGH THE PREAMBLE, LET US LOOK AT HOW OUR CONSTITUTION CAME TO BE WRITTEN.

On 9 December 1946, about eight months before India became independent, a group of men and women met in a beautifully decorated hall in New Delhi, which is now known as the Central Hall of Parliament House. They were there to discuss their ideas and write the Constitution.

Because they had gathered, or assembled, to write the Constitution, they were called the Constituent Assembly. They had many meetings and discussions, and almost all of them came up with ideas to put into the Constitution. But writing or 'drafting' a constitution is a special task, and so they chose a smaller group of people from among themselves to do this. The leader (or Chairman) of this Drafting Committee was Dr Bhimrao Ramji Ambedkar. It took two years, eleven months and seventeen days to fully discuss and write the Constitution.

There are three original copies of the Constitution. One was handwritten in English and beautifully illustrated by a number of artists, led by Nandlal Bose of Santiniketan. The second was also in English, but printed. The third was handwritten in Hindi and illustrated by a different group of artists. These are kept in a locked glass case under controlled temperature in the Parliament Library in New Delhi. Other copies can be seen elsewhere, for example in the India International Centre Library and the Nehru Memorial Museum and Library in New Delhi.

WHO WERE SOME OF THE MAKERS OF OUR CONSTITUTION?

DR RAJENDRA PRASAD

He was born on 3 December 1884 at Jiradi, a village in Bihar. He was a bright student and won a gold medal in law. He was influenced by Gandhiji and was active in the independence movement. He was the President of the Constituent Assembly. He became the first President of India and served for two terms. He died on 28 February 1963.

Each President is elected for a term of five years. Dr Rajendra Prasad was the only President to be elected for two terms. We have had Hindu, Muslim and Sikh Presidents. In 2007, for the first time, a woman became President.

PANDIT JAWAHARLAL NEHRU

He was born on 14 November 1889 at Allahabad in the United Provinces (now Uttar Pradesh). He went to school and college in England and became a lawyer. After returning to India, he joined Gandhiji in the independence movement. When India became independent in 1947, he was chosen to be the first Prime Minister. He continued to serve as Prime Minister till his death on 27 May 1964. He worked very hard to make India a better country and was called the architect of modern India. He was very fond of children and was known affectionately as Chacha Nehru. His birthday is celebrated as Children's Day.

Jawaharlal Nehru talking to children of farmers during his visit to areas near Delhi which had been affected by hail-storms.

Pandit Nehru's daughter, Indira Gandhi, also became Prime Minister of India, as did his grandson, Rajiv Gandhi.

DR BHIMRAO RAMJI AMBEDKAR

He was born on 14 April 1891 at Mhow in the Central Provinces (now Madhya Pradesh). His father was in the British Army. Ambedkar overcame many difficulties in order to study. He and some other children were made to sit outside their classroom, away from the others, because they were from a caste that was considered 'untouchable'. The teacher did not help them or look after them. They were not even allowed to touch the jug of water kept for other children to drink.

Ambedkar first went to Bombay (now Mumbai) and then to England and the USA to complete his studies. On his return to India, he practised law. He always remembered how unfair and difficult life was for people who were 'untouchables' and he fought against the caste system which caused this. He believed deeply in equality and fraternity and was a great force in the writing of our Constitution. He was the first Law Minister of India. In October 1956, he became a Buddhist. He died on 6 December 1956.

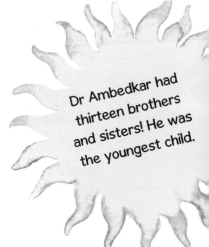

Dr Ambedkar had thirteen brothers and sisters! He was the youngest child.

SARDAR VALLABHBHAI PATEL

He was born on 31 October 1875 at Nadiad in Gujarat. As a young boy he worked in the fields with his father. He worked hard to educate himself on his own and became a lawyer. He was inspired by Gandhiji and organized the farmers of Gujarat in non-violent movements against the British. He was the first Deputy Prime Minister of India. He persuaded more than 500 princely states to join the Indian Union and because of his strong character was known as the Iron Man. He died on 15 December 1950.

MAULANA ABUL KALAM MUHIYUDDIN AHMED

He was better known as Maulana Azad, and was born on 11 November 1888 at Mecca (now Saudi Arabia). His father was a very learned Muslim scholar. Maulana Azad was a journalist and established an Urdu weekly. His pen name was Azad (which means 'free'). He was a great supporter of Hindu–Muslim unity. He said, just as a Hindu can say with pride that he or she is an Indian, so can a Muslim or Christian. He was the first Education Minister of India. He died on 22 February 1958.

> The Bharat Ratna is India's highest award for persons who are not in the armed forces. It is in the shape of a pipal leaf. Till 2015, forty-five Bharat Ratnas have been given, of which only five have been awarded to women. The six men described here were each honoured with the Bharat Ratna, in some cases after they had died.

RAJKUMARI AMRIT KAUR

She was born on 2 February 1889 at Lucknow in the United Provinces (now Uttar Pradesh). She was a Christian. She went to school and college in England. Upon her return to India, she was influenced greatly by Gandhiji and worked closely with him for many years. She became Health Minister, the first woman to be a minister in independent India. She worked hard to get rid of customs like child marriage and the purdah system (where a woman is, for example, made to cover her face or not move much outside the home). She wanted girls and boys to be treated equally and for all children to be able to go to school. She died on 2 October 1964.

CHAKRAVARTI RAJAGOPALACHARI

He was born on 10 December 1878 at Thorapalli, a village in the district of Salem (in Tamil Nadu). CR or Rajaji, as he was called, studied in a small town and later at Presidency College in Madras (now Chennai). He was active in the independence movement and worked hard to improve the lives of 'untouchables' or Dalits. He was the only Indian Governor-General and led a very simple life in the grand building now known as Rashtrapati Bhawan, washing his own clothes and polishing his own shoes. He was a great believer in world peace. He died on 25 December 1972 at the age of ninety-four.

The Constituent Assembly approved the Constitution on 26 November 1949. (This came to be known as Law Day, but is now observed as Constitution Day.) It was signed by 284 members of the Constituent Assembly on 24 January 1950.

Two days later, on 26 January (which is known as Republic Day), we began to be ruled by the laws of the Constitution of India. This was exactly twenty years from the day that Jawaharlal Nehru had demanded 'Purna Swaraj' or complete Independence from the British.

Republic Day Parade: a float showing dolls from West Bengal. Parliament House is in the background.

Now that we know what the Preamble says and about the people who wrote it, here it is again in simple words but in a very long sentence. I have replaced the word 'people' with 'children'.

WE, THE CHILDREN OF INDIA, having taken a firm decision to make India an INDEPENDENT DEMOCRATIC COUNTRY that will provide a BETTER LIFE for all Indians; that will not make any religion more important than any other, and will RESPECT ALL RELIGIONS and BELIEFS; and will make sure that all of us:

are treated FAIRLY AND HONESTLY;

are FREE to think and to act, and to practise a religion or belief of our choice;

are EQUAL and are given the same chances to make our lives better;

and will encourage among us LOVE AND RESPECT for each other, so that we stand united and care for our country;

NOW GIVE TO OURSELVES THIS CONSTITUTION.

WHAT NEEDS TO BE DONE?

It is now sixty-six years since we got our Constitution, but we still need to work hard to fulfill the promises it made.

The Constitution gives every Indian child the right to food, health and education. However we have children in India who are poor and hungry. Some are ill. Some do not know how to read or write. Some are forced to work. How can we be equal and free if our brothers and sisters are not able to get a better life? We must be fair and honest and try to improve the lives of ALL.

Gandhiji once said, 'Be the change that you want to see'. If we want to change others around us, we have to first change ourselves, and be as good, kind, just, honest and brave as we want others to be.

We must make sure that we all help and love each other, so that our India is indeed a peaceful and happy place. We should also take care of the places we live in or visit—from our villages and cities to our forests, lakes and rivers. Then we can all say with pride, 'Sare jahan se acchha Hindustan hamara'.

FINALLY...

In order to help you remember the spirit of the Preamble, here is a short poem.

Let's be equal, just and free—
Strong in our diversity:
Free in thought and free in prayer,
Free to dream and free to dare,
Free to love and free to care.
Let's be equal, just and free—
Strong in our diversity.

Let's be equal, free and just,
Unified in love and trust:
Strong to lend the weak a hand,
Strong to help and understand,
Strong to build a happier land.
Let's be equal, free and just,
Unified in love and trust.

This drawing is by Nandini Seth